'He is a poet

on the page,

is his blazing vision of the life

behind this one, the life we ought

to be living and are not.'

MICHAEL FEINGOLD

'The strength from which all else flows

is the passion for love, the unquenchable

lust, the yearning for connection with

the Other that defines the language

and the form and the almost tropical

feverishness of Kondoleon's plays.'

DON SHEWEY, *THE VILLAGE VOICE*

polari plays

Published by Polari Plays, an imprint of Polari Press.

polari.com @polaripress

ISBN: 978-1-914237-25-6

This edition was first published in the UK in 2024.

Cover design and typesetting by Peter Collins for Polari. Typeset in a custom typeface by Bijou Type and Roslindale by David Jonathan Ross. Printed on responsibly sourced paper using vegetable inks.

harry kondoleon

christmas on mars

The AIDS Plays Project

The AIDS Plays Project is re-staging and re-publishing the theatrical works of writers whose lives were cut short by HIV/AIDS-related illnesses. Striving for cultural recovery and repair, the project seeks to mend the connection between these trailblazing writers and a younger generation of queer artists and audiences.

Director: Alastair Curtis

theaidsplaysproject.com
@theaidsplaysproject

Christmas on Mars *was revived by The AIDS Plays Project at London Performance Studios on 9th December 2023. The cast, in order of speaking, was as follows:*

BRUNO   Dominic Holmes

AUDREY   Mary Malone

NISSIM   Nathan Armarkwei-Laryea

INGRID   Sharon Small

Creative Team

Director Alastair Curtis

Set and Costume Design Max Allen *and* Elliott Adcock

Music Helen Noir

Producer Izzy Parriss

Creative Production Katie Byrne *and* Max Laurie

Photos clockwise from top left:
Sharon Small as Ingrid;
Dominic Holmes as Bruno;
Mary Malone as Audrey; Nathan
Armarkwei-Laryea as Nissim
Photos © Tyler Kelly

x

a flaming creature

Theatre critic and writer **Don Shewey**
remembers his friendship with Harry Kondoleon.
October 2023

ALASTAIR CURTIS: Could we start by discussing your relationship with Harry Kondoleon?

DON SHEWEY: I was a theatre editor and critic in New York City when we met in the early 80s. I saw *Self Torture and Strenuous Exercise* in 1981 and wrote a review about it. He then invited me to one of his plays at Yale, where he was studying at the time. It was called *Rococo*, a two-act play that is not done very often now, but that production starred none other than Frances McDormand. Shortly after, in 1983, there was a festival of his short plays at John Jay College, New York. I interviewed him for the *Village Voice*, in a piece called 'Ferocious Fairytales'. After that we got to know each other and stayed close friends until he died.

How would you characterise his writing style?
He was a comic writer primarily, with a touch of surrealism and zaniness. When I wrote about him, I put him in the lineage of Joe Orton, John Guare and Christopher Durang, who took naturalistic forms into the stratosphere. Harry was also a man of letters, a culture vulture from a very early age. He read a lot and loved film. He was a painter and poet. He pulled all of

that into his work, which could be original and florid. From
the beginning, when he still was an undergraduate, he won
playwriting awards every year in school. Right off the bat, his
voice was so singular, poetic – and queer, too. He was a little shy
about being openly gay. At some point he gave that up.

What films and literature was Harry inspired by?
He loved European art films, Antonioni and Godard especially.
He loved following the Andy Warhol crowd and Patti Smith.
He enjoyed poetry by Anne Sexton and particularly Sylvia
Plath. He once said: 'William Shakespeare – that's my husband
in heaven.' I said, 'Who's your husband in hell?' He said, 'Oh
there's so many.' He could be very funny.

**He had a gift for one-liners. One of my favourites in this play
is when Ingrid calls Audrey a 'witch on an iceberg.'**
He was such a character. No one who met him could ever forget
him. It's like how people talk about Oscar Wilde. He was a
dandy, always impeccably dressed with some quirky accessory.
Handsome too, with very expressive eyes. A flaming creature.

There's a beautiful photograph of him in drag as 'Coco'.
She was a trip! Those pictures were done by his friend Tom
Holdorf, sadly no longer with us. Coco was a character Harry
created especially for the shoot. He loved being photographed
and photographers loved to photograph him because he was
so photogenic.

PHOTO: THOMAS HOLDORF

I actually discovered Harry through Peter Hujar's portrait of him from 1983.

That's a beautiful portrait.

It's absolutely gorgeous, isn't it?

I don't know how it happened but I do know he was pleased to be shot by Peter Hujar, whom he admired. He's looking at himself in a hand mirror. That's very much Harry!

Do you have any memories of *Christmas on Mars* and its premiere?

It was a fantastic production, starring many people who went onto big things. Michael O'Keefe, who played Bruno, was a film actor best known for *The Great Santini*; he's gone on to star

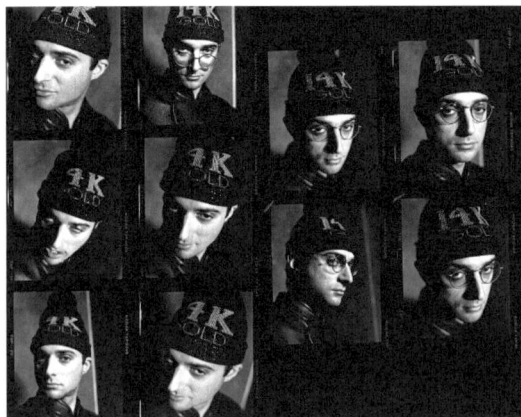

PHOTO: SEBASTIAN LI

in numerous TV shows and films. Harriet Harris, who played Audrey, has become a successful character actor. Joe Pichette, who played Nissim—alas, no longer with us—worked a lot in the Play-House of the Ridiculous with John Vaccaro at La MaMa. He was a terrific actor!

Did he ever talk to you about the play's conception?
His best friend was Stephen Soba, now his literary executor. When I told him you were doing this, he said: 'you can tell him that I remember proudly that I requested Harry write a gay character.' So, Harry came up with Nissim. In the second production of *Christmas on Mars*, in San Diego or Washington, I remember Harry told me that when he went to one of the last rehearsals, the actor playing Nissim was playing him too camp. Harry said: "No, no, cut all that shit out. He's a real person." The next rehearsal, all that was gone. Harry was very particular about the way his plays were performed.

Do you have a favourite play?

One of the earliest plays I saw by him was called *The Brides*. It's a text that has no set number of characters, so every production is completely different. It can be done with three women, or it can be done with five characters. Sometimes there is a male character; sometimes there is not. I love that play. It's a beautiful poem for the stage.

I saw in *Last Address*, a short film by Ira Sachs, that Harry was living on the same block as the artist Félix González-Torres in West Side Manhattan. Could you talk to me about Harry's relationship with New York over the years?

Well, he grew up in Queens, a very prosaic part of New York City. His family were very Greek, to the extent his father's name was Sophocles and his mother's name was Athena! His family were very connected to their Greek heritage, including speaking Greek at home. Harry has an older sister, Christine, and they have the exact same birthday. They were so smart and arty, more than their parents, who were very square: his father was an accountant and his mother a social worker. Christine, in particular, was a huge ally. She loved him deeply. She was an art historian and curator, now retired.

Harry went to Hamilton College for undergraduate, then moved to New Haven to go to Yale. A few years later he moved back to New York City, to 10th Street in the East Village, which was very funky at the time. The neighbourhood was a little sketchy, lots of drugs on the street and so forth. But Harry liked going to all the galleries, gay bars and performance art spaces that were opening there, such as the Pyramid and Club 57.

He also had a patron named Stephen Graham, whose family owned *The Washington Post*. Stephen and his wife Cathy loved Harry and his plays and they let him move into one of their lofts in SoHo shortly after he was diagnosed with AIDS in the 1990s. It was huge, old-fashioned and big enough that he could literally ride a bicycle around it. Harry's bedroom was like a little house in the middle of it! That's where he wrote *Diary of a Lost Boy* and *Saved or Destroyed*, his final play. But going up and down in that building—it was a freight elevator situation—proved hard as he was getting frailer and sicker, so he eventually moved to London Terrace. It wasn't exactly fancy, but it was a nice apartment building in Chelsea where Susan Sontag and Annie Leibovitz had adjacent apartments. That was where Harry was living when he died.

Sontag, Leibovitz, the Pyramid, Club 57... He was at the centre of New York's Downtown, then. Harry seems always to have been in the right place at the right time!
Well, he was blessed in some ways and cursed in others. He had a lot of people on his side, but he also knew how to piss people off and make enemies.

Enemies? Tell me more.

One of the regrettable things is that Harry never found one
director he connected with. Christopher Durang had Jerry
Zaks and, later, Nicholas Martin. Sam Shepard had Robert
Woodruff. Harry never had one director. He could be a little
difficult to work with. The lead actor of *Zero Positive*, a play he
wrote in 1989, was well-known, but Harry thought he was wrong
for the part and fired him during the show's previews. The
director, an actor and friend of theirs, also quit. It was turmoil.
But I remember Harry saying afterwards, with no regrets:
"playwrights have a lot of rights, and I exercised mine."

**You mention he was writing a couple of novels in the last
years of his life. I know about *Diary of a Lost Boy*, which
was published in 1994 a couple of months before Harry
passed away. Were there others?**

He wrote another beautiful novel called *Human Nature*,
which never got published. It's a dreamy story about a
woman who goes to a retreat centre for people with various
kinds of sicknesses, spiritual as well as physical. There is a
page missing which is a problem, but I would love to have it
published. Who knows if that will ever happen?

**For those readers coming to Harry's work for the first time,
which plays should they try and read next?**

I would recommend *Self Torture and Strenuous Exercise*, his
book of selected plays. That contains his brilliantly funny

one-act play *Self Torture and Strenuous Exercise*, as well as *Anteroom*. A favourite play of mine is *Play Yourself*, which was only performed posthumously. It's about a former Hollywood starlet named Jean, loosely based on Louise Brooks, who has long retired from show business when an obsessed fan shows up on her doorstep. It's very Bergman-like and a fantastic role for an ageing actress. Estelle Parsons did a reading once, and Janice Rule starred in a workshop version on the West Coast. It deserves to be much better-known.

With all your experience seeing these plays firsthand and knowing Harry as closely as you did, is there any advice you would give to our actors?

Don't push the laughs. Play it very straight-faced. The humour will come. As with Joe Orton, you can do the characters overbroadly but they are not as fun that way. Remember these are real people. Play them as naturalistically as you would a Eugene O'Neill character. Harry also felt a kinship with the plays of Tennessee Williams. His characters can be outlandish but inside they are real people. So, finding the essence of the person is key. They are not farcical or satirical. Harry saw them as fairytales.

Is there anything else you'd like to add?

For the actor playing Nissim, I will say this: the character is really a portrait of Harry. Like Nissim, Harry loved babies. He was obsessed by them. In his heart of hearts, he would have loved to be a father. His sister Christine had a son named Lucas, who is a grown man now, and Harry loved him to death. You know, Harry was a big pop music fan—I used to make mixtapes for him—and his favourite song was 'Song for a Future Generation' by the B-52s because of the line 'let's meet and a have a baby now.' He loved that.

Don Shewey is a theatre critic and editor from New York City. He runs harrykondoleon.com, an online archive and tribute to Harry Kondoleon. As a journalist and critic, he has also published three books about theatre and written hundreds of articles for The New York Times, The Village Voice, Esquire, Rolling Stone, *and many other publications.*

Alastair Curtis is a writer and director from London.

Christmas on Mars

by Harry Kondoleon

CHRISTMAS ON MARS *was first presented by Playwrights Horizons, in association with New York Theatre Workshop, at Playwrights Horizons on 2 June 1983. It was directed by Andre Ernotte; the setting was by Andrew Jackness; costumes were by Rita Ryack; the lighting was by James F. Ingalls; and the production stage manager was J. Thomas Vivian. The cast, in order of speaking, was as follows:*

BRUNO	Michael O'Keefe
AUDREY	Harriet Harris
NISSIM	Joe Pichette
INGRID	Marie Cheatham

Characters

BRUNO *30, good-looking.*

AUDREY *27, pretty.*

NISSIM *30.*

INGRID *47, Audrey's mother*

Time

Act One: July.

Act Two: December.

Setting

The large main room of an apartment in a city.

The room is completely bare. The walls are painted a very pale pink. In Act Two the room remains bare except for the addition of a skirted bassinet.

In the original production of the play, midstage left and right were two windows. Up center in the room was an archway and beyond it a hallway running off left and right to the other rooms of the apartment. Directly up center of the archway was the front door.

Content warning

Contains infrequent use of discriminatory and ableist language of the period.

Act One

BRUNO   I've written a letter to your mother.

AUDREY   I hope you're joking.

BRUNO   Don't get excited, I wrote her a short harmless little note.

AUDREY   What kind of note? Harmless? We're talking about a woman who stuck me with a fork and threatened to pour boiling water over my face. How could you write to her?

BRUNO   Listen to me for one second, please, will you? I wrote to her for a very practical reason. Now, first of all, you yourself said you're not frightened of her anymore, right? What happened happened ten years ago, right? And nothing like it's happened since.

AUDREY   That's because I ran away from home. You know all this, why should I have to repeat it and suffer?

BRUNO   Audrey, I'm the last one to make light of pain from the past, I've had my share but everyone has, everyone's had some bad time at one time or another growing up, but that's the whole point of it.

AUDREY   How did you get her address?

BRUNO   I wrote her the shortest little note. I said that you and I were in love and looking for an apartment and in fact had found one.

AUDREY   This one?

BRUNO   That's right.

AUDREY   This one? But I only saw it for the first time
today. And you told her we found one?

BRUNO   But I knew you'd love it and you do, we both
do — you know what this city's like, people kill each
other for apartments — we've got to decide here and
now today to take it or leave it and we can't leave it
because I'll tell you, I've been the only one looking and
I haven't found anything this good or anything half as
good or anything really at all else. This is it. We pay this
month's rent, two months' security and sign the lease by
sundown or lose the space completely.

AUDREY   You've written to her for a loan?!

BRUNO   In a way. Do you think they're going to let us
sign a lease with our skittish income? The landlord
works with credit raters — they want someone with
a credit rating and money in the bank. We need your
mother to sign the lease in her name, yes, and to make
a small loan — I have no savings, do you? This is our
chance to move and move quickly. Do you think I like
living with a roommate at my age? And how much
could you enjoy the broom closet you use your entire
salary to pay for? Let's swallow teenage pride, Audrey —
you'll feel better for it — we went out to dinner with my
parents, didn't we, even though they're both hopeless

yahoos — it wasn't so awful. You've spoken on the telephone with your mother a few times, this is just another step.

AUDREY   After all these years of struggling independently I don't want to ask for her help.

BRUNO   You don't have to. You haven't asked, I have. When she walks in all you have to do is smile, I'll do all the talking.

AUDREY   She's coming here now?

BRUNO   Yes, to see the apartment and sign the lease and then we'll have it – we'll have the apartment. We'll move in and be happy here together.

AUDREY   You just assumed I'd like it and want it.

BRUNO   You do, don't you? You do.

AUDREY   Yes, I do. I do like it.

BRUNO   You see, Bruno's not such a bozo, is he? Is he? Am I?

BRUNO *tickles* **AUDREY**. *They kiss.*

AUDREY   There's something I should tell you, Bruno. I've been putting it off for several months.

BRUNO   Shoot.

AUDREY   I'm having a baby.

BRUNO   A baby?

AUDREY   That's right, a small one.

BRUNO   Our baby, yours and mine?

AUDREY *(Rolling her eyes)* No, mine and the President's.

BRUNO   A baby! A baby! *(He laughs, delighted)*

AUDREY   Does it make you happy?

BRUNO   Happy? I'll say! And how! A baby! Audrey, you aren't joking, are you? No, of course not! A baby! It isn't anything I've thought about but I suppose it's something I've always wanted and thought about without knowing it. A little baby, to hold and play with and dance around. Happy? — I'm ecstatic — of course this means we can marry — we will marry — you'll marry me won't you? — I sound like a fool — Audrey, I love you, will you marry me? Say yes quickly. I love you, we'll be happy, we'll take the apartment, I know we'll be happy.

AUDREY   This is the only room that gets any sunlight. I can't imagine sticking a baby in one of those dark small rooms off the hall.

BRUNO   This could be the nursery, why not? It's the first room you enter: anyone who would be coming to visit would be coming to see the baby anyway and there it would be when the door swings open. We could put the cradle right here.

AUDREY   And we'd take one of the small dark rooms for ourselves?

BRUNO   Yes! Why not? We'll be so happy we won't notice.

AUDREY   And the rent?

BRUNO   Happiness itself will pay the rent!

AUDREY *(A joke)* We can't afford it.

BRUNO   That's not true. If I get that cologne commercial my income will triple and you'll probably get a promotion just for recommending me.

AUDREY   If, maybe, when and perhaps.

BRUNO   Don't be negative, say yes.

AUDREY   You've got the job, I know it.

BRUNO   Really?

AUDREY   Positively. Marian Free told me this morning.

BRUNO   Fantastic! And you're to thank I know and I will, on my knees in utter thanksgiving from now until doomsday, say yes, you'll marry me and we'll take the apartment.

AUDREY   And you're happy about the baby?

BRUNO   Should I do a somersault?

AUDREY   I'll marry you.

BRUNO   Sound a little more enthusiastic or I'll reconsider.

They have a long kiss. The buzzer rings, they part alarmed.

That must be her — so, everything's cool, right? We're getting married and about to start a new family, a perfect time to make up with your mother, right?

AUDREY   I'm not afraid. What difference does it make, I'm adult now. You're right, I should see her, prove to myself she has no power over me anymore.

BRUNO   That's right.

A knocking at the door.

AUDREY *(Quickly)* You're not to tell her about the baby —
promise me — she'll use it as an excuse to throw herself
at me, I know her.

BRUNO　　Don't worry, I'll do all the talking.

BRUNO *opens the door.* **NISSIM** *enters. He is thirty, slightly
pudgy, wears an airline steward's uniform and carries a
flight bag.*

NISSIM　　Well, here they be, the happy couple.

AUDREY　　This isn't my mother.

BRUNO　　Sometimes I think it's mine. What are you doing
here, Nissim?

NISSIM　　Hello, Audrey, that is your name, isn't it? I don't
suppose Bruno's told you about me.

AUDREY　　You're Bruno's roommate. You're an airline
steward.

NISSIM　　That is correct.

BRUNO　　Nissim, what are you doing here? Please go.

NISSIM　　I have a very interesting letter with me, Audrey,
would you like to see it? It's from Bruno. But perhaps
you two composed it together, I don't know.

BRUNO　　Aren't you supposed to be in Timbuktu or
something?

NISSIM　　I quit.

BRUNO   You what?!

NISSIM   I quit my job. Tell me, Audrey, how well do you
know Bruno, just how well?

AUDREY   We're lovers.

NISSIM   Oh you think so.

AUDREY   We sleep together frequently.

NISSIM   I know that! We should start our little talk
— Bruno, you may stay or go, it's not consequential —
Audrey, you should sit down, what I tell you may shock
and disturb you, I don't want to catch you off guard.

AUDREY   There's no place to sit.

BRUNO   Are you determined thoroughly to play the fool
or are you going to leave this apartment now?

NISSIM   Well, you can lean against the wall if you need to.

AUDREY   What exactly are you talking about?

NISSIM   I'm talking about sex — S-E-X, love and sex.

AUDREY   Good. Go ahead.

BRUNO   Nissim, go home and we'll talk when I get there,
all right? We're expecting Audrey's mother any minute
and it would make things unnecessarily difficult if you
were here.

NISSIM   I don't doubt it. I'm talking of things, Audrey,
perhaps unfit for a mother's ears.

AUDREY   Like what?

NISSIM   Isn't it obvious?

AUDREY   No, not really. Give me a hint.

BRUNO   She's laughing at you, Nissim.

NISSIM   Bruno's told you perhaps that Bruno and I have lived together for many years.

AUDREY   You were roommates all through college and roommates again after that when you moved to the city.

NISSIM   That is correct. Don't you find that a little strange?

AUDREY   No. Bruno's led me to believe you've been very dependent upon him.

NISSIM   Led you to believe? Oh, Audrey, we don't know each other very well but I'm going to have to call you naive. Well, better you should discover it before the ceremony. Here it is, you asked for it: Bruno and I are lovers.

BRUNO (*Shocked, incredulous*) What? You and I are lovers!

NISSIM   And have been since the minute we met.

AUDREY   So? Why would I care about a thing like that?

NISSIM   Well, you ought to!

BRUNO   Nissim!

AUDREY   I don't care.

NISSIM   Audrey, I don't think you've fully comprehended what I've attempted to reveal to you.

AUDREY   You say you two are lovers — great.

NISSIM   We do *homosexual* things together!

AUDREY   Fine.

NISSIM   Don't you maybe see this as an interruption in your relationship that makes it impossible to go on?

AUDREY   No, I don't.

NISSIM   Well it is! I know no one takes gay people very seriously but this is very serious. I tell you, I'm standing between the two of you.

AUDREY   But it doesn't bother me. I had a lesbian attachment once. I had it severed.

BRUNO   Satisfied now, Nissim? Go home.

NISSIM   Okay, so you're not shocked—

BRUNO   Shocked about what? That I nurse a lunatic without remuneration? I'm the one who's shocked. How could you invent such an infantile lie?

NISSIM   So, you're not shocked, Audrey, because I have no concrete proof, I understand that and am sympathetic to it so I'm prepared to amend my argument so that I might present tangible documents for that is what you obviously require and here I have them. Letters! *(He has removed a bunch of letters from his flight bag)*

BRUNO   What the hell are you doing with those?!

AUDREY   Letters?

NISSIM   Oh, well, something elicits a response, thank God. Yes, letters! Long feverish letters written perhaps in states of undress. Letters written to your so-called lover Bruno whose real name, by the way, and hasn't he told you, is Elliot — Elliot Frankel! Bruno Ward is a made-up name! Getting shocked? Hard to believe so many letters could arrive at the same address to a made-up name but here they are!

BRUNO   I thought this brand of espionage was something only mothers of teenagers practiced.

NISSIM   Teenagers? Oh yes, there are more than a few from them. Here's one whose message spills out onto the envelope, "Let's get closer, all risks involved."

BRUNO   Give me those!

NISSIM   Get away from me — they're for Audrey. Take them, Audrey, take them and commit them to memory.

BRUNO   Now we're going to watch you flip out, is that what's next?

NISSIM   Planning on renting this apartment together? I'm sure it's not large enough, not for Bruno and all his little friends, his "affairs" or whatever you call it. Here's one from a top model — why not? — encloses a photo of herself in an Italian magazine — this so-called fashion model wants to be a dog — that's a departure that ought to perk you up — according to this letter she runs around her apartment on all fours barking while Bruno holds her leash and pours dried dog food in a bowl. Have you ever noticed the tooth marks on Bruno's ankles? "I fell," he says. Since when do the floors have teeth? If you can call this an affair I don't know how you can pretend to know the names of anything. I guess then you can

give everything a new name. I could be a model too if I
were a little younger and better looking — a woman at a
party told me I could be in *GQ* — and she was drinking
club soda the whole time.

BRUNO   You could never have been a model. You're too
short and your skin isn't good.

NISSIM   That's right, throw that in my face!

BRUNO   Why don't you look at yourself realistically?

NISSIM   Why don't you die? I am beautiful! I was! And
if I'm not it's because you made me ugly: you not loving
me! That's what's brought me any ugliness I have so you
have no right to say so.

BRUNO   Can't you see that you're a nuisance here? Can't
you see Audrey is bored by you?

NISSIM   She's in shock! You're in shock, Audrey, aren't you!

AUDREY   No, no, actually I'm not.

NISSIM *(Rifling through the clutched letters in panic)* Not
shocked by these?! Read them! Can't you read? "I want
you to come in me until there's no place left to go!" "You
are the only one I love!" "I love you more and more all the
time!" "I'm yours!" "Yours truly!" Look at these letters!

AUDREY   Why? What do they prove?

NISSIM   That he doesn't love you!

AUDREY   If that's true why would he ask me to marry him?

NISSIM   That's a question you should ask yourself!

AUDREY   Neither of us are virgins. I expected Bruno to—

NISSIM   Not Bruno! Elliot! Elliot!

AUDREY   Elliot, Bruno, what difference does it make?
I expected him to have had many affairs. Certainly
you've had—

NISSIM   No, I have not!

AUDREY   I'm sure—

NISSIM   You're wrong!

BRUNO   Now you see what we're dealing with here.

NISSIM   No, not completely. There's more to the truth, a
simple fact. Bruno's only interested in you to advance
his career. Did you hear me? Don't you ever change your
expression? He's using you! He's a model and an actor.
You work at a commercial casting office, figure it out!
When he's through with you he'll drop you like a hot
potato!

Pause.

AUDREY *(Calmly, to Bruno)* Is that true?

BRUNO   Of course it's not true.

AUDREY   There.

NISSIM   Oh? This is cute! "Is that true?" "Of course it's
not true." And that's it. You make a very interesting
couple! Don't you care — about *anything*? I see. There's
some silent bargain here. Some bargain with lies and
compromises. That's what it is, isn't it? I can smell it, the
lies. The lies and the compromises. And the doubleness.

The perpetual doubleness. Ten years alias Bruno, have it your way, and I are friends and once, once in ten years I'm introduced to his parents. We meet for lunch, it's Easter. I'm told not to be flamboyant, to strive for the subdued. The fact is I'm always subdued! It's only when I have the doubleness to face, the craven doubleness — the hypocrisy — the — the — inscrutable hypocrisy, that's when I become flamboyant. I walked here from across town — walked in shoes a half-size too small and to begin with not designed to walk further than the cab to the doorman — all my shoes are a half-size too small and filled with pain. I wear them deliberately like Christ's thorn hat to remind myself of the doubleness and the falsehood.

BRUNO   You sound like a rag doll going mad.

NISSIM   You mean a fag? I'm not afraid of being called a fag. Asshole! I choose to be frivolous! Oh God let something frivolous come to my mind! The pain and execution of my feet in these shoes — that is not frivolity! Where is the beauty of the soul? I ask the question and get ridiculed. This century the beauty of the soul has diminished like a shrunken head. *(Throwing down the letters to the floor)* Take your filthy letters! We're through! I hate you! I have driven myself to places of sickness and distraction in the name of love. In the name of understanding I have stopped understanding everything! I have let go of so many things!

BRUNO   You hold on to grudges.

NISSIM   And you begrudge me that one small luxury! You've granted yourself every possible excess with your dick-crazy girlfriends — me, not even this one tiny concession. I don't dare review the shocking shopping list of predilections these sordid letters reveal lest I gag and expire. *(Spoken at even higher speed)* I will not give up my soul, rather than that I'll give up love — if that's what this is — God knows I've awakened in the night asking myself — tortured again with the duplicity, the malign duplicity of all things and don't ask me what I mean.

AUDREY *(Calmly)* I know what you mean.

NISSIM   I've gone beyond it all. I swallow transgression now like water. I wake up in the morning and I feel like a contusion — banged around in the night, blue with the truth.

BRUNO   Nissim.

NISSIM   Don't even breathe in my direction! As a baby I rolled my eyes behind my lids. I was intolerant of everything, especially of those larger creatures who hovered over my crib and playpen with their fake concern and shrill voices. As an adolescent I sat alone inventing characters for myself — anyone to play with in my misery, making the arabesque connections common only among the insane and gifted: I stunned and isolated my peers, divorced couples flew to my side for advice and comfort, time and again I— *(He faints to the floor)*

BRUNO   Well, that put a lid on that.

AUDREY   What happened?

BRUNO   I thought he was going to tell every episode of his life image by image.

AUDREY   Is he okay?

BRUNO   He faints like that a lot, whenever he gets excited. It's his system's way of saying "Enough." I hope you don't believe everything he says, he's an hysteric.

AUDREY *has picked up a letter to read.*

What's that?

AUDREY   It's the letter he walked in with, from you. It says we're getting married. It was written ten days ago.

BRUNO   So?

AUDREY   How did you know we were getting married? You just assumed it?

BRUNO   Well we are aren't we? Right? I don't see how the letter changes anything. I thought he could use the interim to adjust to the fact, you see how he is about me. I wonder how hc got fired.

Enter **INGRID**. *She is attractive, forty-seven and nicely dressed.*

INGRID   Hello, Audrey.

AUDREY   Hello, Ingrid.

BRUNO   Hi, I'm Bruno. Did you have any trouble finding the building? Well, it's the only one with the awning and it doesn't really look like the others. Did you notice the little angel faces on the entablature?

INGRID   Yes, hard to tell whether they're angels or monkeys.

BRUNO   Oh, you're right! But that's the charm of them, don't you think so?

INGRID   How've you been, Audrey?

AUDREY   Fine. I've been fine. I'm expecting a raise.

INGRID   Good.

AUDREY   Yes, it is good, I like my work and I'm good at it.

INGRID   Well, you're very smart and pretty and have charm so there's no reason why you wouldn't be successful at anything you set your mind to do.

AUDREY   Okay, that's enough! We all know why we're all standing here. Bruno's written some kind of letter to you — I know all about it — he's pleaded in some degree or another for a loan and some signatures so that we might secure this apartment. It wasn't my idea — you know better than that. But now that you're here, fine, agree to help or go. If you help we'll pay you back and thank you, if you don't, that's fine too, we'll make other arrangements. I'm just not willing to mystify this meeting into Mother's

Day or some such other event of reconciliation. I'm my own woman now and have been for a long time and I'm proud of myself.

INGRID   Audrey, I just want to—

AUDREY   No — don't want to — don't want to anything, because I'm not prepared to deliver and I don't want a scene!

BRUNO   Audrey, can't we just take this step by—

AUDREY   No, Bruno. Ingrid and I understand each other very well. There's no reason for you to mediate.

INGRID   Who's that?

AUDREY   A friend of Bruno's.

INGRID   Is he sick?

BRUNO   Yes.

INGRID   He's resting?

BRUNO   In a way.

INGRID   Is he a soldier?

BRUNO   A flight attendant.

INGRID   Isn't there anything we could do for him to make him more comfortable or get him to a doctor?

BRUNO   Oh, he'll come to in a minute or so.

INGRID   Give me a little time, Audrey. Just give me a little time.

AUDREY   I don't know what you're talking about.

INGRID   I want to make up for some things, things from the past.

AUDREY   I don't know what you're referring to.

BRUNO   Audrey—

AUDREY   Shut up, Bruno, I'm talking to Ingrid!

INGRID *(With difficulty)* I want to patch up the past, Audrey. I want you to say you'll give me half a chance.

AUDREY   In other words you're saying you don't want to help us with this little housing problem?

BRUNO   Audrey.

NISSIM *sits up slowly as if from sleep.*

NISSIM *(Not rushed)* People think I'm fruity, they don't know my parents were the fruity ones. My mother was a translator and my father an inventor, both frustrated artists — they got into a knife fight and killed each other — drinkers, they tried to instill in me a faithlessness in the future. They called me Nissim — Hebrew for miracles and neither of them Jewish. You must be Audrey's mother. Every Christmas it was the same story with them, "There is no God, there is no Christmas." Cheapskates using ideology as an excuse not to go shopping. After burying my parents I went under the care of two aunts — two complete racists who were in charge of hiring and firing in the city school system. Anything my parents didn't accomplish in the way of screwing me up for life these two hellions finished up but totally.

INGRID   Hi, I'm Ingrid.

NISSIM   Hi.

INGRID   How are you feeling?

NISSIM   Not very well, thank you. Your outfit's pretty but the scarf doesn't go.

INGRID   I worked once in the garment business and the insignia on your uniform is a lot like the one we used.

NISSIM   Really? I was fired.

BRUNO   I thought you quit.

INGRID   Fired? Why?

NISSIM   I refused to put ice in the drinks: everything seemed cold enough to me to begin with.

INGRID   That doesn't seem reason enough to me to let you go.

NISSIM   Well, I got airsick.

INGRID   That could have been from something you ate or maybe you were upset about something.

NISSIM   I was upset. I got a letter from my friend Bruno that he was getting married and if he couldn't find an apartment I'd have to move out so she could move in.

BRUNO   Please, is this necessary?

INGRID   No wonder you were upset. And they fired you for that?

NISSIM   I started screaming during takeoff.

INGRID   Oh.

NISSIM *(Holding up an imaginary cigarette between his fingers)* Do you have a light?

INGRID   A light? You don't have a cigarette.

NISSIM   Oh, I've given up smoking real cigarettes, I smoke these. I've gotten back to the original impulse for smoking. Light me up.

INGRID *lights with a real lighter where* **NISSIM**'s *cigarette would be. He exhales and "smokes" the cigarette.*

Thanks. I'm glad I'm out of that milieu anyway. Did you know the stewardesses have sex with the pilots before during and after takeoff? They all make the same fake motor sounds when they come. The stewards work twice as hard as the stewardesses because they all wanted to be stewardesses in the first place. The food's not half-bad.

BRUNO   Ingrid, why not take a look around the apartment. Through that door there's a corridor which leads to some other rooms. The layout's kind of wonderful. It's an old building, in great shape and with lots of character.

INGRID   It's nice. I like it. The other rooms are through here?

BRUNO   That's right. Take a look. It's very special.

INGRID *exits to inspect the other rooms.*

Okay, are you going to leave now or am I going to kick

you out?

NISSIM   I'm not the one who wants to be a dog so don't talk to me as if I were one.

BRUNO   If you make yourself into a ludicrous thing how else can I talk to you?

NISSIM   Where are you going to find someone like me who cooks for you?

BRUNO   I don't exactly call mixing yogurt with a tablespoon of instant coffee cooking.

NISSIM *(To Audrey, desperately)* It was in a recipe book and it tastes like parfait!

AUDREY   I do it.

NISSIM   Audrey, do you think I'm too fat or too skinny? I try to lose weight to look slender, then I think I'm too puny and I try to gain weight. In an effort to overcome shyness I become grotesquely friendly. I've stopped looking at people. I don't know who's flirting and who's looking in utter disbelief.

AUDREY   I'm sorry, I was thinking of something else, what was the question?

BRUNO   The question is how long are you going to stay a flippo? Don't you see it's your way of not growing up and being a man?

NISSIM   And you — how long will you still rely on your pathetic little career to buoy you up?

BRUNO   Oh, go faint! Audrey, listen to me, let's play this right, okay? The only reason to have your mother here at all was to get her help not to frighten her off.

NISSIM You're very busy in the gym with your weights — why not build up your character, that's the really scrawny side of you. My aunts and parents were lunatics but at least I know up from down.

INGRID *enters.*

INGRID The dark rooms off the hall could be a problem but it's not a bad apartment. When you take into account the size and the way these buildings have appreciated in the last few years, I would even say the price is fair.

BRUNO I'm so glad you like it! I was so excited when I found it. I called Audrey at the office and insisted she zoom right over. As you say, finding an apartment like this in the current market is a minor miracle.

NISSIM *has taken out several sandwiches, a small jar of mayonnaise and a knife to spread it with from his bag. He eats a sandwich.*

NISSIM *(To Ingrid and Audrey)* Sandwich? Sandwich?

INGRID No, thanks.

NISSIM Do you have an ashtray?

INGRID No. *(As a second thought looking through her handbag and removing a sea shell)* Will this do? It's a shell.

NISSIM   Oh, I don't want to use that, it's too good, doesn't it have sentimental value?

INGRID   I don't want it to anymore. Please, use it.

NISSIM   Thank you. Sure you don't want a bite? No-cal mayo. I have six snacks a day and then I take these appetite suppressants.

BRUNO   If you're not going to go, please stop talking.

NISSIM   It's easy for those without appetite to mock the hungry.

INGRID   I've felt that too.

NISSIM   I'm a physicist really — I graduated as a physicist in college.

BRUNO   You did not. You never even graduated.

NISSIM   So I dropped out the month before graduation, what difference does that make? I was an honor student. The dean had me on his list.

BRUNO   Ten minutes ago you said you were going to be a model, now you're a physicist.

NISSIM   So? Brains and beauty can't go together in your mind?

BRUNO   They can but you're not particularly brainy or beautiful.

NISSIM   I need this?

INGRID   You two sound like an old married couple.

BRUNO   Yeah, well, you know, old friends are like old couples.

INGRID   I do like this apartment. A lot.

NISSIM   I like it too. And I'll be needing a place.

BRUNO   What?

NISSIM   The old one will remind me of us.

BRUNO   What us, there is no us! Ingrid, please ignore this person. He's been trying to pass himself off as something more than my burden in order to prevent Audrey and me from marrying. You know, it's one of those friendships you make when you're too young to know better and then spend the rest of your life trying to shake.

INGRID   I like him.

BRUNO *(An about-face)* He's my best friend, I'm not saying anything bad. I'm just trying to make everything clear so you get the right picture.

INGRID, *on cue with* **NISSIM**, *who barely indicates he is about to have another "cigarette," gives him a light.*

NISSIM   The right picture, Ingrid, is these two don't care a button for each other but think they do or want to think they do or something even more insidious I'm too pooped to imagine.

INGRID   Audrey, is this true? Are you just marrying for no reason? Are you in love?

AUDREY   What's it to you?

INGRID   You're my daughter. I love you.

AUDREY *(Violent)* Oh, please! Won't you spare me?!

BRUNO   We do love each other, of course! What other possible reason nowadays would provoke two people to marry? We are in love. We love each other.

AUDREY   My mother's a very practical person, Bruno. She'll appreciate and understand us for speaking more directly to her.

BRUNO   What do you mean?

AUDREY   Oh, why pretend anymore, Bruno? It is rather silly, all this the sky is blue and I love you — better we should drop it now, as Nissim says, before the ceremony. Let's admit that when we sign the contract we're doing just that — signing a contract. She's not going to help us, can't you see she's thinking of getting the apartment for herself?

INGRID   If this is honestly the way you feel, Audrey, you shouldn't be marrying.

AUDREY   Oh no? Why? How big a difference will it make from your marriage, the one that lasted two weeks, the one with my father? Were you so in love?

INGRID   No, obviously we were not. We were friends.

AUDREY   Oh, friends. Well, Bruno and I are friends too.

BRUNO   We're more than friends, Audrey, what are you trying to do?

AUDREY   Please, Bruno, I'm talking to Ingrid now.

BRUNO   So I've disappeared? You're just trying to drive her off!

NISSIM *(Holding up half a sandwich)* A half?

AUDREY   Bruno and I understand one another. We're a
lot alike, I knew that the minute I met him. I expect our
marriage to last more than two weeks, two years, two
hundred years, what difference does it make to you?

INGRID   Audrey, I never married your father, I made that
up. We were friends, and I wanted a baby so we had one.
He met some woman and went off and married her.

AUDREY *(Frightened, violent)* Do you think I want to hear this
now?

INGRID   So we tipped our hats or whatever we had on our
heads at the time and said so long. He was not interested
in having children. At the time I didn't think that was
the best cradle talk so I weaved a tale of divorce — it was
the best I could come up with at the time — there was no
divorce, it was invented for your benefit, Audrey, to make
you feel less lonely and have more to tell your friends
when asked where your father was. I didn't think it would
turn on me and you would grow to hate me.

AUDREY   Liar.

INGRID *(Takes a letter out of her bag)* When you were a baby
I wrote to your father that he should at least visit you at
holidays and set up some form of communication and
he wrote back this letter. Take it, it's all made very clear.
Read it.

AUDREY   An old letter. Oh, this is good! What does it say, that he didn't care to see me? You've told me as much, what do I need to read? Isn't this convenient? It seems today everyone has a letter of some kind to produce at some key point and foul up other people's lives, some nasty and concise little letter. Keep it! You've kept it this long, keep it, I don't want it.

INGRID Take the goddamn letter, Audrey! I won't be blamed for your father anymore — you hate him? Go to him with it, seek him out, the return address is on the envelope — it hasn't changed, stalk his building, attack his wife, defame him, scar him if you can but please forgive me at last won't you, can't you?

AUDREY *gingerly takes the letter, holds, doesn't open it.*

AUDREY Are you stupid? Do you think you're going to walk in here with some yellowed prop from the past, distort the truth and reinstate yourself in a role you can't possibly have? You'd have been better off signing the lease and bribing us with the security deposit. Now get out!

BRUNO Audrey, you're really overdoing it.

AUDREY Shut up!

INGRID Please, Audrey.

AUDREY Get out! You didn't want me as a baby and I don't want you now: get out!

INGRID Who said I didn't want you? I did. I did always. Give me a chance, Audrey — if I was a bad mother give me a chance to be a better one — I'm begging you!

AUDREY   Don't touch me! *(She rips up the letter violently)*
Don't you dare touch me! Do you really think I'm going
to let you have another chance at me?

INGRID   Audrey, please, I love you.

AUDREY *screams as if hot oil has been thrown upon her and
exits running to the corridor and bathroom.*

NISSIM *(After a pause)* Maybe I should go after her and help
her. I have some onboard fresheners with me and a
comb. *(He remains on the floor)*

BRUNO   Maybe this wasn't such a good idea after all, you
coming here. I didn't realize she'd be so… I guess people
don't ever recover from things like child abuse.

INGRID   Child abuse? What do you mean?

BRUNO   I mean Audrey's told me how things were with you
growing up. I'm not here to pass judgment. I'm just saying
it must not be easy to recover from those kinds of scars.

INGRID   What has she told you?

BRUNO   Oh, there's no reason to list the things here and
embarrass one another, you know what they are.

INGRID   Tell me. Tell me what she told you.

BRUNO   What, is this guilt-and-punishment day? You
know what things you did! Beating her with an electrical
cord, sticking her with a fork, pouring boiling water over
her head.

INGRID   She told you I did these things?

BRUNO   Well you did! Didn't you?

INGRID   No. Never. I've never hit Audrey. I've never even
shouted at her.

BRUNO   I don't understand. She told me the whole time
she was growing up you beat her with objects until she
couldn't stand it anymore and ran away from home.

INGRID   No.

NISSIM   You mean it's not true? She made it up?

Pause. INGRID *doesn't answer. She's obviously in great
turmoil, wanting to speak, unable to speak. Pain, shame
and anger rising conflicted to the surface, it shows in her
face and speech: she loses her warm and cool composure
and comes apart.*

INGRID   No, I never hit her. Something worse. It's worse.
So much worse. I'm so ashamed, oh God! I feel so low, so
low for so long, I can't stand up.

NISSIM *(So softly)* What happened?

INGRID *(A pipe bursting)* I fell in love! *(Drowning)* I fell in
love, I fell in love. With a man. A man appeared. I'd never
believed in love like that, to be taken up like that and be
erased completely. I forgot my name. I only knew I loved
him and would walk into fire for him. He was jealous.
Didn't believe Audrey's father wasn't a lover. He never
said so but I think he resented Audrey. *(Gagging)* He

hated her. He wanted me to go away with him. Audrey was just a little girl at the time. I left her with my sister. It was temporary I thought. Today is the first time I've seen her since.

NISSIM *(Softly)* What happened to the man?

INGRID   What? What happened? Look at me. Look at my face!

BRUNO   I should check in on Audrey, see if she's all right. *(He doesn't move)*

INGRID   I had a business at the time, another business. He made fun of it and borrowed money from it, not to gamble or anything like that but to supposedly live better. He was sort of a philosopher. He didn't work. I neglected the business, it fell apart at both ends, the money ran out. We began to fight all the time. This is ridiculous to tell. And then he left me. It's ridiculous!

She stops to cover her face, crying, half-laughing at herself. She is a little bit frightening. **NISSIM** *hands her a tissue.*

I couldn't get up! An old woman who lived at the hotel I was staying at came in twice a day to feed me. I couldn't even clean myself. I sat all day in a chair near the door with my suitcase like a dead person. At night I made phone calls. I talked to myself. People hung up on me. I cried so much I couldn't breathe. I wanted to die! I'd left my child for this man.

BRUNO   What did you do?

INGRID   I made a lot of money. It seemed like the only
           alternative, that or die. I started another business.

NISSIM   A few years ago I hypnotized myself into
           believing I was a bisexual or something and I married a
           girl. She was a junkie. We were happy briefly I think. She
           disappeared eventually but not before we attempted to
           adopt a child. It was the whole reason we came together,
           to enhance our chances of getting through the initial
           application period. They told us there was a paucity and
           when we pressed them further they sent us runaway
           teenagers, you know, that city program where you keep
           them in your home until they remove everything with
           any resale value and then run away again. I taught
           kindergarten for six months. I wanted all the children
           to love one another but every day it got more and
           more obvious they would grow up to be criminals like
           their parents. *(He rises from the floor)* I'm going to help
           Audrey. It's my job. Ingrid, if you go out for anything I
           need another pack of cigarettes. And don't get them in
           the lobby the price is inflated.

BRUNO   What difference does it make where she doesn't
           get them as long as they're imaginary?

NISSIM   That's no reason to get gypped. *(He exits)*

INGRID   He's in love with you, you know.

BRUNO   I know, my cross to bear. I've been his support system for the last ten years! True, there was a brief respite when he married that fellow maniac. Next to her he seemed like the rock of ages. Stoned and haywire. In one of her less aphasic hours she ranted to me how I was responsible for the way Nissim was and therefore he was my responsibility. Do you think that's so? I don't really think anyone's really responsible for really anyone. It's true I became friends with Nissim out of maybe a spurt of vanity, knowing I could by association make even a misfit like Nissim an insider. Colleges are like that. Actually, the whole world is like that. I've always been good-looking and traded upon it. Do you find me good-looking? When I was a baby my mother told me I looked like a munchkin and that my brothers were better-looking. My mother has this theory that if you're good-looking you can get anything you want out of the world and if you're not you can expect nothing. The idea sounds grotesque but experience seems to confirm its truth. My father manufactured sports equipment for children. That's how I got started. I hit balls with bats, threw them into hoops and kicked them toward end zones, in black-and-white and then in color. I was the only kid on my block with an income. I was despised and idolized. My brothers thought it too sissified to model. Anyway, as they grew up they got more and more horselike. They're partners now and sell pharmaceuticals. We don't communicate. You're very pretty, actually, prettier in a lot of ways than Audrey. My hair's not as thick as it used to be. There's a thickness under my eyes and a spider of lines near my mouth. My parents were good-looking, in a way, but cruel and stupid also. As they've gotten older they've lost their looks and have become jolly and inoffensive.

INGRID has picked up a handful of the letters strewn on the floor and reads aloud at random with no intonation, as if reading a foreign language with good to average skill.

INGRID   "It's night now, my husband's asleep in the other room. When he touched me before, I shut my eyes and pretended it was you and trembled. Are you thinking of me now, Darling?" "You asked me to send this, with it I send my arms, lips and tongue, kiss this letter after you read it — I'll feel it down here. Until I see you I remain your love slave in escrow." "When you talk to me in bed it ends the unbearable silence of existence."

BRUNO   I thought it might be exciting to reread the letters long after parting company, to give myself a rise when my hair goes white. And this shell? It's that guy's, isn't it, your lover? Something you found together on the beach, right? Or something you picked up as a reminder the day you decided you'd cried enough and weren't going to cry anymore. And at night when you feel weak you hold it up to your ear and cry anyway because it reminds you of the sea, but really the sound it's just air, right? *(Holding the letters and the shell, he opens the window)* Who needs them, right?

He throws them out. The shell falls silently away and the letters, caught by some wind, fly up and away before he shuts the window again.

INGRID   Hold me. Hold me. Please. Just for a moment. Please hold me. I'm so lonely. Lonelysick down into my guts. Just for a moment. Hold me.

BRUNO *embraces* INGRID. *He kisses her on the mouth. She shudders and weeps.*

BRUNO   What's wrong? Don't worry about Audrey, she'll come around. You'll see, the baby's going to make all the difference in the world.

INGRID   What did you say?

BRUNO   I said once the baby arrives everything will be —

INGRID   *(Seeing the first ray of light after years of darkness)* Say it again!

BRUNO   What, that Audrey and I are having—

INGRID *falls to her knees at* BRUNO*'s feet.*

INGRID   Please, please.

BRUNO   What's wrong?

INGRID   I'm willing to do anything, anything.

BRUNO   What's got into you?

INGRID   All I want is a part, just a part.

BRUNO   A part? A part of what?

INGRID *(Faster than her regular speaking)* I did such a botch-up job with Audrey, she'll never forgive me and why should she. I'll take the tiniest and darkest room off the hall, you won't even know I'm living here I'll be so quiet and invisible. All I ask is that I be allowed near it, to hold it and kiss it because I love it already, I do, I love it with all my heart and I want more than anything to feel my heart again, to feel something — I want to feel joy! In exchange, in exchange I'll of course pay for the apartment, I'll pay all the rent, the utilities, the furniture, anything — Audrey will have to take off from work — I'll supplement her salary and wait on her — you can take fewer jobs, pick and choose the ones you like, quit altogether if you like — this is the chance I've been looking for, the chance to live again!

AUDREY *and* NISSIM *enter hand in hand.*

NISSIM   Audrey and I have exchanged face-washing techniques and have become fast friends.

AUDREY *(To Bruno)* Why is she on her knees?

NISSIM   You can get up now, Ingrid, Audrey forgives you.

AUDREY   I didn't say that I—

NISSIM   No! Audrey, now! What did I tell you in the

toilet? To say you forgive is three-quarters of forgiving.

AUDREY   But I didn't agree with you.

NISSIM   Hush! To forgive is to be at one with the season of rebirth. Don't you want to be at one with spring?

BRUNO   It's July.

AUDREY *(To Bruno)* You told her didn't you? You told her.

NISSIM   Told her what? Where did my ashtray go?

INGRID *(Still on her knees)* Audrey, I want to help. I want to make up. I'll do anything you want, I'll be anything, just don't shut me out, not now, not at this time.

NISSIM   What time? What does she mean "this time"?

AUDREY   Nissim, I didn't tell you in the bathroom but I'm pregnant.

NISSIM   A baby. A baby? Not a little baby, a little thing, a baby, no.

AUDREY   Yes.

NISSIM   A baby. But, Bruno, is this true, your baby? Tell me Bruno, your baby?

BRUNO   Yes! Yes, Nissim!

NISSIM   A baby! *(He falls to his knees to pray)* Oh merciful God who has taken this time to shed light on this miserable and thirsty soul, one thousand thank-yous, from this day on I walk in a state of gratefulness and if I should stray from gratitude please kill me in my path, I love you so, yours, Nissim.

AUDREY   The baby is mine. It belongs to me.

NISSIM   Tell her, Bruno. Tell her. Bruno, tell her.

BRUNO   Tell her what?!

NISSIM   About the baby, your first baby. About the knife, tell her.

BRUNO   I don't know what you're talking about.

NISSIM   Oh no? Look everyone, look! *(He opens his shirt and reveals a gash with stitches)* My scar — twenty-four stitches. How did I get twenty-four stitches and not very far from my heart? Seven years ago May fourth Bruno and Nissim go out for ice cream — out from the bushes springs a devil, hissing for money! We hand over our wallets, "Good evening, Unkind Sir, do have a sporting time somewhere with our money, bye." *"I want those watches! Give me those watches!"* We hand over the watches, lose what time we may, he got the watches. Not enough, he spots Bruno's ring and says, *"Hand it over!"* "No," shouts Bruno. "No!" Well, no apparently is the magic word. *"No? No?"* Out comes the knife ready to cut Bruno's face. I throw myself between Bruno and the knife, holding my own knife, my mayonnaise knife. His knife cuts my chest, my knife cuts nothing but we all run into the night on our own. At home Bruno says he will give me anything in repay, for saving him. Twenty-four stitches and nearly I lost my life! Promise me your firstborn.

BRUNO   Enough! When eccentricity dances over into the certifiably insane it's got to be put a stop to!

NISSIM   You promised me!

BRUNO   Well, I didn't mean it! I meant it as a form of speech, as a hyperbole for my gratitude. I never even expected to ever have a child.

NISSIM   It's mine. The baby is mine. I earned it. It's promised to me. I'm sorry, Audrey, I'll make it up to you.

BRUNO   He thinks he's Rumpelstiltskin! You're a nut! A nut! A hopelessly cracked nut!

NISSIM   I am not a nut. I am inviolate and holy. The baby is mine! Mine!

BRUNO   Is this going to be another fit scene, Nissim? Isn't it someone else's turn?

NISSIM   I'm sorry, Audrey, try and understand me — what my life has been like — I wasn't cut out for it — I'm too pure — it's all too sordid, the world — I can't go on without it, without the baby — when every magazine ad mocks me, every TV plot and commercial, every store window telling me what I want is not normal, is not a romance, is upside down and warped and then, as if all this treachery heaped on me were not enough — I have *him* who embellishes every day with still another betrayal, another degrading episode recorded in letters. What sin in the name of sexual contact haven't you committed — have you even read your own letters? Where are they? Where'd they go?

BRUNO   You're just repressed, Nissim, that's why you're

so easily derailed by things which wouldn't upset a
twelve-year-old.

NISSIM   I'm repressed? You're the most repressed person
I know! What's more repressed than promiscuity?

BRUNO   Won't you ever get tired of jabbering?

NISSIM   No, only of the lies, villain! The baby is mine!

BRUNO   Stop saying that!

NISSIM   The baby is mine. My soul is in that baby.

BRUNO   Well get your soul out of it but quick!

NISSIN *(Resolute)* It's my baby. I'm having a baby.

BRUNO   We should have you taken away.

NISSIM   Take me away, you've taken everything else
from me — what haven't you taken? Tell them, Bruno,
how you come into my room and steal everything.

BRUNO   I never stole anything from you.

NISSIM   Nothing tangible — but nothing valuable ever is.
I broke all your mother's dishes, Bruno — I did.

BRUNO   What!

NISSIM *(To Audrey and Ingrid)* They had a Birds of Paradise
pattern on them and for years those birds have been
mocking me, squeaking up from the soup or salad,
"You'll never get to paradise." I couldn't take it anymore
and I smashed each one against the wall. If there's no
paradise how can I go on? How can I wake up and face
all the animals in this zoo?

BRUNO   I'm going to break you in half!

NISSIM *takes out his sandwich knife and holds it up.*

NISSIM   Stay away from me! I can wield a knife too you know! Who wants to be cut first?

INGRID   Nissim, you can visit the baby whenever you like, you can be the godfather, that would be good.

NISSIM   I've grown so sick of musty reassurances — I've had so many! For kindness I've had to sink and sink and sink! I'm sick of kindness, of tiny kindnesses taking up space nibbling at everything and leaving me starving.

BRUNO   Put the knife down, Nissim. Put it down.

NISSIM   You will have to kill me before I forsake it! Better I should die at my own hand than waste away from despair!

AUDREY *feels, for the first time, a movement from the baby. She is alarmed and excited and lets out a sound.*

AUDREY   I feel it! I feel it, the baby.

NISSIM, *shocked and alarmed, also touches his stomach, feeling a sympathy pain. He lets out a sound and faints.*

BRUNO   Here we go again.

Curtain.

END OF ACT ONE

Act Two

Five-and-a-half months later.

BRUNO Can this go on? No, not really, not if you think about it for more than five minutes. Your mother being here half makes sense — she's supporting us and she'll be able to help with the baby. But him? How many babies can we nurse at one time? And he's going to be a bad influence on that baby, that's a fact. We can fool ourselves into thinking otherwise but let's face it: he's emotionally unstable, overneedy, overbearing, hyperactive, talkative. I mean sit down and really ask yourself do you want a son or daughter who acts like him? No, of course not. And we can't afford him. He brings in no income. You're not working anymore, I'm working less frequently now. Your mother's made some remarks about expenses suggesting there's a limit to what she has in that account. We just can't afford the extra mouth to feed! On top of all this, and you know this, he loves me. Think what that's like for me, Audrey, the strain of it. Before at least the admissions were repressed and avoidable but now that he thinks *he's* having the baby he thinks we're all married to each other! He's having a bad effect on you too, Audrey.

I know you're not fond of this topic lately but *when are we going to get married?* I'm not complaining, not at all, I know it must be a big strain to carry around a developing baby for nine months — more than nine months, the doctor says you're drastically overdue — and that a man can't begin to imagine what it must be like but I don't think it's so much the baby that's come between the intimacy between the two of us, but him. You know what I'm talking about. Should I get you a chair? I can get you a chair.

AUDREY   No.

BRUNO   I'm talking about us making love — you don't want to do it anymore and you won't talk about it and I know why, this is some offshoot of his whole celibacy-trip isn't it? The doctor says there's nothing wrong with intercourse during pregnancy so what's the problem? The problem is him, him right down the line because he's moved in here and more or less taken over your mind. You don't listen to me. You don't listen to your obstetrician. You listen to him, the doctor of hysteria. Can't you see he's on the fast track to nowhere? We can't sit down and plan our lives with a tag-along, it makes happiness a complete impossibility but happiness — and can't you see this? — is anathema to him! He's happy unhappy! Have you ever seen him make any attempts to meet anyone, to find someone?

We can't have him preying upon our lives indefinitely
— he can visit anytime — we said he could be godfather
— what else could he expect? Today we tell him. Do you
understand? Before the baby arrives I want him out!

NISSIM *(Offstage, jubilant)* Everyone close your eyes, I'm
coming in.

BRUNO   We're not closing our eyes so just come in.

NISSIM *enters with shopping bags, packages, and a beautiful, real, evergreen tree.*

NISSIM   Isn't it the most beautiful, the most perfect
tree? I hunted like a maniac and then suddenly just
as it was getting dark, this one reached out and picked
me. This is the first year I wasn't too depressed to go
tree-shopping. Usually I skip it altogether or attach
some branches and a star to the TV antenna. Smell the
tree, Audrey.

BRUNO   Nissim, Audrey and I have been having a little
talk.

NISSIM   I bet I know what you've been talking about.

BRUNO   I bet you don't.

NISSIM *gives* **AUDREY** *a bag of chestnuts. She eats them.*

NISSIM   I brought you those chestnuts. Have you had
your nap yet? Did you eat the lunch I left you? How
are you feeling? Do you think you might have it today?

Bruno, you were going to get out the tree stuff while I was gone.

BRUNO   Nissim, I'm bringing a chair in here. Audrey wants to sit.

AUDREY (*Eating chestnuts*) I don't want to sit.

BRUNO   Well maybe I want to sit! This chairlessness is ridiculous!

NISSIM   Bruno, please, let it pass one day without this argument.

BRUNO *exits.*

I saw Marian Free shopping this morning. She sends her regards, says she'll never forgive you for not attending your baby shower and wasn't going to mail you the presents but did anyway and not to expect them right away because she didn't send them first class. I made up a good reason why you weren't seeing anyone and that it wasn't personal or anything.

AUDREY   Bruno says you'll be a bad influence on the baby, that we can't afford to keep you, that you're having a bad effect on me and that he wants you out.

Not moving, **NISSIM** *considers these things for several moments. He decides not to let this information change his good mood.*

NISSIM   Wait until you see what I got Ingrid, it's

gorgeous. I know you haven't had the energy to shop so I
bought presents for you to give out. They're wrapped so
I'm going to have to tell you what's in everything.

AUDREY   No more nuts?

BRUNO *enters with an old, red-painted, iron Christmas-tree
stand, a box of small, colored, electrical bulbs, their wire
and a small stepladder.*

BRUNO   Here. I can't find the ornaments. I don't even
remember if there are any.

NISSIM   Your parents must have had ornaments. If they
gave you all this stuff they wouldn't keep the ornaments.

BRUNO   Maybe they broke them, I don't know, leave me
alone.

NISSIM   I guess I could make some. String popcorn or
something.

AUDREY   We have popcorn?

NISSIM   Audrey, it's time now for your nap.

AUDREY   I'm not tired.

BRUNO   No, Nissim's right, time for your nap, go on.
Besides, Nissim and I need time to talk together, go on
Audrey.

NISSIM   I'll put an eggnog on your night table so when
you wake up you can have it.

AUDREY *exits.*

BRUNO   The tree's very nice, Nissim, but think how much
           happier you'll be when you have your own tree in your
           own place. Won't that be great, a place of your own?

NISSIM   This is my home.

*Still talking, without thinking they put up the tree. Clearly
they have performed many tasks together: one holds, the
other one tightens the screws.*

BRUNO   Temporarily it is but not forever, you knew that
           when we moved in, we agreed to it, right?

NISSIM   You said the apartment was temporary
           inasmuch as you one day wanted to buy a house when
           your career took off and you made a lot of money.

BRUNO   But that house, if ever I purchased such a thing,
           would be for Audrey and myself, not you. We're a couple,
           Audrey and I. As a couple we'd be better off living alone,
           together. Do you understand?

NISSIM   You mean without Ingrid?

BRUNO   Yes, eventually, without Ingrid and without you.

NISSIM   How about the baby? Would that be included?

BRUNO   Nissim, listen to me, I think it would be best if
           you moved.

NISSIM   I don't want to move.

BRUNO   I know you don't but I think you should. I'd help
           you look for a new place, I'll help you paint it and fix it
           up, whatever.

NISSIM *has been testing the bulbs to see which light and which don't.*

NISSIM   The red ones are the only ones that work. They remind me of a street in Amsterdam where all these lonely people sat in windows with red lights on them.

BRUNO   So what do you say, the day after New Year's we do a little apartment-hunting for you? Who knows, maybe we'll even find something in this building. Please be cooperative.

NISSIM   I am cooperative, I know I am because I've been trying with every drop of my being. You're afraid I'll frighten the baby and be a neurotic influence upon it. Can't you see how hard I've been trying, how, out of sheer will power and hope for the future, I've cured myself of so many things — smoking, fainting, fits? I am not moving.

BRUNO   Don't you miss your job? You could go back to it.

NISSIM   Back to the sky? I was fired, I quit, there's nothing for me there anymore.

BRUNO   Well what do you expect to do to earn money? You think you're just going to sit around here and be nanny?

NISSIM   Maybe I'll get a job like yours selling things.

BRUNO   They're not going to put someone like you in a commercial to advertise their product.

NISSIM   Why not?

BRUNO　　Why not because Nissim you are from outer space and no one would ever drink the beer you chose or the cereal you poured in the morning.

NISSIM　　You just want to see me that way.

BRUNO　　What's to become of you, Nissim? Don't you ever give that any thought?

NISSIM　　If I stop thinking I can stop thinking you don't love me and think then that the baby will love me in the way no one and nothing has ever loved me.

BRUNO　　It's unnatural to put so much hope in one baby — what if it's retarded or deformed?

NISSIM　　Do you really think something like that would bother me? I'd love it any way it arrived.

BRUNO　　Go out and try to meet someone, will you try? Will you? No, you won't even make that small effort. Can't you wear clothes that are more flattering or at least fit? For example what the hell are you wearing? Is that supposed to be a maternity shirt or what?

NISSIM　　It's Vietnamese.

BRUNO　　What's to become of you? Ask yourself!

NISSIM　　It's true I don't spend every waking hour grooming myself and exercising and shopping for clothes. I guess I'm just a bad person! My teeth are good. They're straight at least. But they aren't the trouble, are they? The trouble is you don't love me.

BRUNO　　That's right! I don't! I don't love you in the way you mean, in the way you want me to.

NISSIM   But you do love me.

BRUNO   No I do not! We just covered that.

NISSIM   You do, you just lack the self-knowledge to
know it.

BRUNO   Okay, Nissim, you want love, let's love. That's
what you want, come on, let's love. Take off your things.
There's lots of room on the floor, we can love right here.

NISSIM *(Frightened)* Stop it.

BRUNO   Stop what? Love? Stop love? I love you, right?
So let's do it, lover! Come on!

BRUNO *is assaulting* **NISSIM**.

NISSIM   No, don't, please.

BRUNO   No don't please what? No, you don't want love?
No? It's all you talk about all day, have some! No? Then
what kind of love are you talking about, Nissim, do you
even know? You don't love me, you just love someone
who you know can't return it so you have this protracted,
stunted-adolescent crush! Coward! Watching you watch
me out of the corner of your eye for the last ten years
wondering if ever you'd find the courage to make a move
— just to get it over with once and for all and out of the
way! But you never did, did you? No, all your energy is
funneled into casting spells and deceiving yourself —
weakling! GET OUT OF MY LIFE!

Enter **AUDREY** *holding a rubber baby doll wearing an absurdly applied diaper.*

AUDREY   Somebody put the diaper on the practice doll wrong.

NISSIM *(From the floor)* Why did Bruno become my friend at all, Audrey, have you ever wondered? It's not a very difficult question. Because I flattered him. Said things to make him feel better, said them every day with loving regularity, said the things I wished in my heart some voice, any voice, muttering out of the darkness might say to me, bright comments and boosters to face the day with and believe myself special — yes I'm expert in these forms of speech — I just pretend he's me in a happy dream and then I just say how good-looking he is, how special, how smart and talented and apart from the others. And when he modestly chimes in, "Oh no, I'm not," I say, "Oh but you know you are." Who wouldn't like a friend like that? Who doesn't need an excuse, any excuse, to believe himself special and apart from the lump of humanity?

BRUNO   All right, stop already.

NISSIM   Stop what?

BRUNO   Audrey, go back to bed.

NISSIM   Audrey, reevaluate, because I think you should, your choice of Bruno as the father of your baby. He doesn't love us. He doesn't love anyone. He doesn't even love himself unless of course the light is hitting him in some interesting way and he happens to pass a mirror. When you get right down to it he'd just as soon everyone drop dead. That way he could be left alone with his mirror. Well, let him go there, to his friend the mirror. Friends, Audrey, are very fickle things, aren't they? One day they need you the next day they don't. Marian Free mentioned in passing they're killing the cologne commercial and that other thing is going off the air as well but said if anything came up she'd give him a call. Funny, I don't hear the phone ringing.

BRUNO   Don't try to frighten me! I can get a job any day of the week if I wanted one, as if it were such a great thing to work!

NISSIM   Think, Audrey, is this the man for your baby, a man who will twist it, seek only his own image in it and misapply the diaper?

BRUNO   Look, I'm sorry.

NISSIM   Sorry about what? That Christmas comes but once a year — we knew that already! I love you, it's a humiliating situation. I would love to not but I can't. Maybe I'll meet someone tomorrow in the lobby and forget about you but I doubt it.

BRUNO   Audrey, tell him how his presence here is making it impossible for the two of us. You say you love me, well, I love her, can't you be sympathetic to that?

NISSIM   Yes but I need things too! I don't really want
to roll over and die as you might have me do. I need
Audrey. I need Ingrid. I need their friendship. I always
thought I needed you, I don't know why. And I need the
baby, something to sink myself into.

BRUNO   That's just it, you want to sink yourself into this
blank infant — why not give it half a chance to develop
into what it might.

NISSIM   Why immediately assume I'll warp it? Why
not believe I have something beautiful to tell it, games
to play and lessons to teach? The baby will love me
instantly, I know it as I know my name and you're
jealous in advance knowing the baby will shrink from
your touch, run screaming from you into my arms!

BRUNO   See what I'm talking about, Audrey? With all the
problems in the world I'll be damned if one of the first
things I'm going to expose my only son or daughter to is
a psychopath.

NISSIM   So, I'm a weirdo, so what? Do you think if you
repeat it often enough I'll become ashamed and change?

BRUNO   I never should have applied to that school.
Better I should have joined the army.

NISSIM   You should have. You've never done anything
for me anyway except maybe make me feel more lonely
and stupid.

BRUNO   You're only attracted to jobs you aren't cut out
            for, to people who can't love you, places you can't get to
            and situations in which you don't fit in!

NISSIM   Maybe you're right but then people like you
            are always encouraging people like me to be weak with
            faulty loans of strength.

*During this altercation the rubber doll has been pulled apart
by the two men.*

BRUNO   What's wrong with you, Audrey — talk!

NISSIM   She's sick of you that's what's wrong — I mean
            right — that's right, we're all sick of you, Bruno.

BRUNO   *SHUT UP!*

NISSIM   Does Audrey know you've been fucking her
            mother?

Pause. NISSIM *attaches the string of unplugged red lights to
the tree. Enter* INGRID *with shopping bags filled with many
wrapped packages.*

INGRID   It's four below zero thank God it's warm in
            here. You're not going to believe what I bought, it's all
            too good. Everything's wrapped but I don't think I'm
            going to be able to wait until tomorrow, it's ridiculous
            to be so excited, I feel like a little girl but then I
            haven't done anything for Christmas since — well, I
            can't wait — this one's for you and Bruno, Audrey —

open it — *(Paying no attention to the lack of glee, she excitedly opens the large wrapped package)* — look! Is that corny: big wrapped box with envelope inside? Open the envelope. *(She opens the envelope)* Tickets! Two tickets for you and Bruno, Audrey. It's for a vacation, are you excited? The whole idea is to fight postpartum depression and the best way to do that is a holiday on the beach! I can take care of the baby so there's nothing to worry about, hotel reservations too. Right now you can't imagine wanting to leave the baby that quickly after it's born but you will, believe me, and the trip will seem a godsend. What happened to the practice baby? *(She quickly sticks the head back on the body while talking)* And this box here and I'm not going to open it is one of the ones for the baby. Look at the elves on the wrapping paper. Oh I can't resist opening it — is this evil? *(She rips open the package)* Look! It's a hat! I'd sell my soul to have a head this small to wear a hat so cute. *(She puts the hat on the doll)* Don't you love it? And this one's for Nissim. *(She opens the present without a second thought)* Look! You don't like it! Of course you don't like it and why? Besides the fact it's misshapen, a wretched color and the wrong size, it was sold to me by a very, minus-the-goatee, handsome clerk, a clerk who when I mentioned I needed to wrap two plane tickets said he was very interested in air travel, said that he loved the uniforms the pilots wear. I said I knew someone who had a uniform very much like that — meaning you. The day after Christmas you put on your uniform and return the pullover. You go to his department with the credit slip in your hand and you say you're interested in mysteries, he's a mystery-story aficionado, you go to his apartment and a little this and a little that and all mysteries are solved. Shave the goatee and he's extremely handsome and I'm not just saying that — I mean not handsome-handsome, but handsome, definitely good. Most of these boxes are for the baby but this one's for me. *(She opens it and laughs: it's a horse's head on a long stick, a toy for children to ride. She rides it)* It's a riot isn't it! But I didn't really buy it to ride. I bought it to copy. I thought I could do a whole line of these things, not horses but the heads of fantastical futuristic animals which is very popular now with children anyway — make them — use bright soft felts and feathers and these little nontoxic sequins — I bought a lot of the stuff already. Just in the elevator I thought of ten places that would carry them, toy and novelty stores, I'm positive I could sell the idea to a manufacturer and the originals of course I would give to the baby — why is everyone staring at me?

BRUNO   Nissim told Audrey that you and I have been together.

INGRID *stops for a moment and then, angry, she slaps*
NISSIM *across the face.*

Serves you right!

INGRID   How could you tell her such a thing?!

NISSIM   It's the truth.

INGRID   The truth in this case distorts the truth. Did you think for a second what good could it do, that it could only upset her!

NISSIM   What about me — I'm not upset? I'm upset to the marrow!

INGRID   Audrey, it's nothing, less than nothing, a few ridiculous afternoons in which I felt a little less lonely and old. No one was trying to hurt or betray you I swear that—

AUDREY   Am I named after a cat?

BRUNO   What?

AUDREY   Am I named after a cat?

NISSIM   What cat?

AUDREY   Aunt Rae told me you had a cat named Audrey and that you named me after it.

BRUNO   This is a ridiculous conversation—

AUDREY   Am I or am I not named after a cat?

INGRID   So, I see, it's back to zero. Because of this insignificant little disclosure. The answer is yes. You are named after a cat, a cat I found.

BRUNO   Audrey, you're getting yourself into a state over nothing, go back to bed.

AUDREY   Your name's Elliot but you never mentioned that until Nissim said it.

BRUNO   I never use that name, what difference does it make?

AUDREY   That's right, none, no difference. My name's Audrey after a stray cat, but then the whole time growing up I never really knew my last name did I?

INGRID   This again too? My last name, his last name, everybody's last name, does it change you, does it mean a thing?

AUDREY   No, nothing means a thing. What ever made you think you'd make such a hot grandmother anyway? Who's to say you wouldn't get bored and walk away, leave it face down in the tub to run out and greet boyfriends?

INGRID   And you, Audrey, what kind of mother will you make? You think you're purifying yourself by chopping us away. You might say I'm the last person in the world qualified to rate motherhood but to me, Audrey, you seem like a witch on an iceberg. Even when you make your sporadic efforts to "understand" I can always feel you backing off and judging, judging everyone. Is it worth it, waiting around for your forgiveness, I've often wondered!

AUDREY   Maybe I'll just go away on my own, alone, away, what's to stop me?

BRUNO   Away where?

NISSIM   Take me with you.

AUDREY   Chicago maybe.

NISSIM   I could show you around I was born there.

BRUNO   You were not!

NISSIM   Just outside of Chicago.

BRUNO   In Miami?

AUDREY   Maybe I'll trip on a step in the snow and crush the baby before I even have it.

NISSIM   No!

AUDREY   Yesterday when I said I was taking the taxi to the doctor I didn't. I didn't go.

BRUNO   You didn't go to your doctor?!

AUDREY   I said I didn't. He handles me like a package that keeps returning. He's jealous of me, of my size.

BRUNO   Audrey, are you going insane?

AUDREY   I went to see my father. That's right, after all this time. I memorized the return address on the envelope you showed me and I went to visit him.

INGRID   Good.

NISSIM   How was it, meeting him?

AUDREY (*Unaffected*) Undramatic. He shook my hand,

brought me a cup of milk and showed me stamps. He said his stamp collection is one of the largest in the United States and I had no reason to doubt him.

BRUNO   I can't talk to you when you go into your dense-style.

NISSIM   Isn't there a Spanish song called "Cuando Cuando Cuando"? Do you know? "Cuando Cuando Cuando."

AUDREY   You thought you were revealing something telling me those two have been at it. I knew that! Like attracts like. And I was never attracted to you, Bruno, not ever, I chose you the way I would a clock or typewriter, something that would efficiently give me something else and you have and here it is. The day I met you I threw my diaphragm onto the train tracks. Here, I said to myself, is a good breeder: good-looking, reasonably intelligent, quick, ambitious, steady-nerved, mature in the relative spectrum of the market and single. How could I be surprised if you revealed yourself base? I've never met a man I haven't found absurd and capable of any baseness.

BRUNO   All right, go inside and lie down, you're just saying things randomly to hurt people and you don't mean any of them.

AUDREY   I do mean them. I selected you, Bruno. Like a salmon. When you came into Marian Free's office I told myself, that's the one. I convinced her to take a second look at your resume. I convinced her — and it wasn't easy — to audition you again when you did so poorly.

BRUNO   Only two things determine whether Marian Free will help you: one, if you call at the right moment, and two, whether or not you are good-looking — if you are she'll walk through fire for you — if you're not you won't get a glass of water.

AUDREY   And you didn't call at the right moment.

BRUNO   I'm going to measure my self-worth from a casting director? It's the kind of job only a child who was never invited to parties would want. Marian Free is a fool! She hasn't a shred of integrity. She's good at casting all right — casting people aside!

AUDREY   She said you were vain and self-absorbed.

BRUNO   And you're not? Confidentially, my dear, Marian Free was going to fire you. She said if you hadn't become pregnant and left she would have asked you to go. The best word she could come up with to describe you was *efficient*, otherwise clients complained constantly of your frosty demeanor and downright charmlessness so don't tell me about Marian Free! And on top of everything else she's a hedgehog.

AUDREY   Was she such a hedgehog when you fucked her last June?

BRUNO   Yes, as a matter of fact, she was. Did it bother you?

AUDREY   No, nor did it the first four times she mentioned
it in the office until on Friday I finally faked tears to
satisfy her and shut her up.

NISSIM   Marian Free?

AUDREY   Don't look so shocked, Nissim, people who are
one way all day are another way all night.

NISSIM   I guess she's a fair-weather friend.

BRUNO   She's an all-weather turncoat!

NISSIM   I put contact paper on all the shelves in the
kitchen.

BRUNO   Who asked you to? No one wants it!

NISSIM   Contact paper is hygienic.

BRUNO   Contact paper is neurotic and Marian Free is a
fool and a hedgehog!

AUDREY   Pick on Nissim, that's handy having always
someone around to spit at so you can feel less tiny.

BRUNO   You told me you ran away from your mother and
lived on your own after she threatened you with boiling
water and stuck you with a fork.

AUDREY   I made it up! I lied! You never saw a fork scar
on my chest did you, Bruno? A child playing detective
would have remarked on the absence but then you never
did look much at my body while yours was there to
choose from did you?

BRUNO   Look, I'm sorry. Can we stop fighting? I'm sorry.

AUDREY   Why? Because the cologne's a flop so all of

a sudden everything smells shitty? There are other colognes, other shirts, ties, suits, robes, pajamas, cigarettes, vermouths and driver's seats to stick your face under or over or beside — or did you expect to merchandise yourself also as a father, or sell the baby itself, sell it up as an image, one more image for your pointless profligacy!

BRUNO   I love you, Audrey, I do love you. I admit I've been shitty at showing it but I'll try harder, I'll be whatever you want me to be.

AUDREY   And my mother? Do you love her too? What a fetching family circle we make: mother, mother, father and friend. And baby makes sideshow.

BRUNO   I said I love you!

INGRID   How can you love someone who's incapable of love? She's never loved anything. If I'm responsible for that so be it. I've tried, I've tried a hundred different ways of being a mother, a friend, a pal, a confidant, a nurse, even a maid. I've failed, you've failed, who cares! I want to move out of here. I wanted to be near the baby to find myself in it and renew my lease on life but I can't stand even another day here watching you isolate yourself further and further until I feel every gesture I make is some absurd call across a mob.

NISSIM   We must believe in love, Audrey — human love — I do, I must, that's all there is on this planet and when there isn't any there's nothing.

AUDREY Love? *(She blurts out a garish laugh)* Love? What love? After some ten years of rubbing my body against others in the dark I'm here to say there is no love. Desire? — certainly. Tenderness? — occasionally. Empathy, kindness, momentary passions, okay, yes, maybe, but no love.

NISSIM *(Punctured by arrows)* No, no, Audrey, don't say that, please, it's so hard for me.

AUDREY Radio and television are mumbo-jumbo, newspapers and magazines are hieroglyphics, billboards and signs are obscenities, and the people in the street caterpillars crawling about afraid always of being squashed. You ask me have I cut myself off from life — *what life?* I'm born for the first time in here! I'm experiencing life from within me — the only place life can come from — I looked for it once in work, in friends, in sex, and found only shadows of those things, squat toneless shadows telling me one day was no different from the last. Do you know of any life out there? Go out and get it but don't bring it back to me!

INGRID No one can do enough for you, Audrey, can they?

AUDREY No, they can't.

INGRID Well then you are going to be a very lonely person, prepare yourself for that future now.

AUDREY You've already prepared me plenty, *Mother.*

INGRID   With that attitude kill yourself now why don't you?

AUDREY   I think of it sometimes, then I think, why
bother? One expects everything to blow up in a minute
anyway, suicide seems redundant.

BRUNO   Audrey, I love you!

AUDREY   Stop saying that to me — it's offensive. You
think I'm ever going to let you fuck me again?

BRUNO   Don't give me this I-fucked-you bullshit because
the same time men are fucking women women are
fucking men!

AUDREY   May I quote you?

BRUNO   And this sarcastic pingpong has got to go. It'll
be bad for the baby.

AUDREY   You are interested only in getting bigger, bigger
in any shape or form possible, and mostly — and isn't
this true, Bruno — it takes the form of sticking your
penis anywhere you can inflate it. Don't ask me if I'm
insane — you are jealous of me, you have been jealous
for months as I've been getting larger and larger and
you've been just some dumb balloon floating around the
periphery of my event. You are all flat and flatness to me
is hideousness. Look at me, I'm full, I'm filled now with
all goodness and purity and I will not let it go, not for
you not for the doctor not for anyone in this world.

She exits. Pause.

BRUNO   What's with her?

NISSIM   Her soul hurts.

BRUNO   And what's this "soul" shit? That's the third
time this week I've heard that expression around here —
is everybody suddenly turning into Emily Dickinson or
what? I told her I loved her what more does she want?

NISSIM   I've felt the way she does, wanting amnesia, to
wake up and forget everything.

BRUNO   Amnesia? As it is you never know where you've
put anything.

NISSIM   Ingrid, did I tell you—

BRUNO   Oh what didn't you tell us?! Have you let
even one minute go by without one of your childhood
recollections?

NISSIM   Bruno, I'm trying to speak in a calm manner so
as not to disturb you.

BRUNO   Disturb me? I told you your very presence
disturbs me!

NISSIM   I'm sorry you feel that way.

BRUNO   She called me a salmon! This is why she
won't marry me — she hates me. She really hates me.
Ingrid, say something, have you suddenly turned into
a zombie — wake up and help me! I'm surrounded by
fools and zombies! Somebody help me! Everyone's had
a flip-out scene why not me, it's my turn — don't I get a
mad scene?

NISSIM   Have it.

BRUNO   *"Have it."* I'd like to have it, with a chainsaw!

NISSIM   Go ahead already.

BRUNO *hollers, stamps his feet, punches the air, kicks the tree, and storms out of the apartment.*

In fifth grade Laurie Ross and Cindy Brooks threw a party, one of those parties where children pet and persecute each other. They made a list of the invitees. Cindy's list fell out of her looseleaf and I picked it up. Next to my name at the bottom was a big question mark. When you have a big question mark next to your name you never fully recover. Wherever you go or whatever you do you have a question mark, it's like having a tail.

INGRID   Maybe we could bring a radio in here and play some music.

NISSIM   Songs on the radio fill me with such longing.

INGRID   There might be a carol on, you'd like that.

NISSIM   They remind me how I can't sing.

INGRID *(Looking out the window between the slits in the Venetian blinds)* So many cabs outside, all rushing to some place. I used to think a cab was something special, that I could just get in one and it would take me away.

NISSIM   I used to think that about airplanes.

INGRID   I've run out of money.

NISSIM   That doesn't matter, Ingrid! I'm going to support us now. I'm going to be a model. Marian said she was going to keep her eyes open for me.

INGRID   What about this man in the store, why don't you arrange to see him, maybe you could meet him.

NISSIM   I couldn't. I'd be too afraid. I've never had the knack of making friends, that's why I became an airline steward.

INGRID   But you might fall in love and run away together.

NISSIM   I couldn't! I can't! You don't understand. I was never a teenager. I never went to beach parties and threw rocks into the sea as if I'd live forever.

INGRID   I don't remember my childhood. Hospitals and gravesites. I rushed to have Audrey. I wasn't yet twenty. I wanted to be related to someone alive.

NISSIM   When I was little I went through a stage where I couldn't go out if my shirt, shorts and socks didn't match. If my shirt was maroon my socks had to have a maroon band around the top and my shorts had to have maroon stripes or maroon in the madras. I don't mean I was upset if these things didn't match I mean I thought the top of the world would fly off and not only myself but all people would be flung into ruin.

INGRID   I'm going away.

NISSIM   Wait, Ingrid, wait a little longer until the baby comes, then we could kidnap it and go away together!

INGRID   I'm not going away alone.

NISSIM　　Not with Bruno.

INGRID　　No. *(Pause)* I met a man. A man in the subway. These plane tickets were for the two of us. I told him I wouldn't go but he insisted I take them hoping I'd change my mind and I have.

NISSIM　　It's a trick! If he's so rich he can run around handing out airline tickets what was he doing in the subway?

INGRID　　He says he likes it, the level of it. His mother just died and left him some money. He said he loved me.

NISSIM　　Oh, Ingrid, listen to yourself! — don't you see it's the same man — the man who left you! — all he did was change his face! He doesn't love you — the baby loves you.

INGRID　　That's the big fishhook isn't it, the baby. One wishes and wishes for so long for something, someone, to arrive and when it does it seems we're no longer fit for it anymore. Don't you see the way Audrey looks at me — and the baby if it looked at me that way I wouldn't be able to stand it — I would die! I'm leaving in the morning. I'll take an airplane to an island I've already forgotten the name of, I know it's hot there and the water around it will be like gin. I'll forget everything, I'll find some other shell, some otherwise ordinary seashell, pick it up and say this is my life now, this moment, this moment with no life before it and no life

after it. It's a laugh isn't it, the new year. What new year?
We never seem to be able to leave ourselves behind, do
we. No matter what surgery we perform the bad limb
seems to grow back eventually. Don't stare at me, it's
enough that I'm admitting any of this out loud. Don't
you think I'd like to rise up out of myself and be strong
— who doesn't?! I've tried to alter my attentions but it's
like a hex, life, the same spells return again and again,
the only thing that changes is your face, every day you
wake up and it's a little more haggard, a little more worn
out, every day the lines of defeat drawn a little more
thickly. Happy New Year.

NISSIM   It's not Christmas yet.

INGRID   Christmas, Halloween, the Fourth of July —
does it make a difference?

NISSIM   It has to! It has to or I can't wake up in the
morning, can't bring my feet out from the covers, it has
to matter, oh Ingrid, it can, we can make it matter! Oh,
I know I sound like a baby but it's true, we can brighten
our own days can't we? We don't have to wake up in a
cloud depressed, desperate, angry, and waiting to die.

INGRID   Make that philosophy work for you.

NISSIM   I can't, not alone, I need to help someone, have
someone help me.

INGRID   You'll find someone like that.

NISSIM   I won't — stay with me, Ingrid! If I've been

getting on your nerves I'll change, I'll be quieter, I'll take
up hobbies, I have the will power, I've proven it.

INGRID   I'm going to my room to pack.

NISSIM   You've lost faith — you can't lose faith! You
haven't been reading the newspapers have you? I told
you not to look at them, it's the same news over and
over — they try to make you think it's some other news
by making it more shocking on alternate days but it's
the same thing and pieced together certainly to make us
lose faith!

INGRID *exits.*

DON'T ABANDON ME! (To himself, red alarm) I mustn't
collapse. I must think of presents and happiness. *(He
picks up the practice doll)* Oh little play-baby, do you love
me? I love you. You do, I know you do. Why don't we
open some of our presents, wouldn't that be fun? It's
naughty but oh let's. What would be in this pretty box,
hard to tell. *(He opens it, using occasionally the forced help
of the practice doll)* A brush and comb set for you, how
nice, but we'll have to put those away for a while until
you're a little less bald. What could be in this big box?
Let's just see. Ooo! A coat with matching little shoes.
Do you like them? Let's just try them on, okay? *(He puts
the red baby coat and red shoes on the practice doll)* How
dashing, how smart! You're a clever baby, ready for school

already but I'll never send you to one of those public torture chambers don't worry or one of those schools named after saints that breed devils. I will teach you everything you need to know. Ask me a question. "Where do babies come from?" From God, little baby. "Who is God?" God is everything good and holy and pure and kind and healthy and growing and generous and good and good and good, that is God, little baby. "And where is he, where is God?" Why God is right above us, little baby, looking down on us. "Why then, tell me, why won't he help us, help us all, even just for a minute?" That's enough questions. We must get on our horse and ride away very fast from these questions, very fast because they will chase us, chase us through the day.

Practice doll in one arm, NISSIM *rides the horse toy, galloping speedily around the room. Enter* AUDREY.

AUDREY   What are you doing?

NISSIM *stops short.*

NISSIM   I'm riding away with the baby.

AUDREY   So am I. I called Aunt Rae and she's coming to pick me up.

NISSIM   Ingrid met a man in the subway and said they were going to fly away together. Bruno left — he had a fit and slammed the door. *(Softly)* I didn't tell you, Audrey

— I didn't want to frighten you, but you can't leave: I'd
have nothing to live for, I'd have no dreams left. You'd
be killing me, Audrey — that'd be on your conscience. I
couldn't go on.

AUDREY   I did a prayer, Nissim. I prayed for the first time
since I was seven. I prayed for the happy answers. I
waited and listened but the angels wouldn't talk.

NISSIM   I have no place to go! My landlord tried to evict
me, he said I was depreciating the building. I'd have to
sleep on a cot in my aunts' hallway — Audrey save me!

AUDREY   My suitcase is packed and on my bed, close it
and bring it out here.

*NISSIM exits. AUDREY sees a gift box under the tree
marked for her. She opens the package. It is a diary.
She flips through it reading a line here and there.
Enter INGRID.*

INGRID   I see you've opened your Christmas present.

AUDREY   What is this?

INGRID   A diary I started the day I left you. I always
intended to give it to you. The first few months I wrote
in it every day, then every few weeks, once a month, the
whole thing trails off in the end.

AUDREY   I don't really like to read.

INGRID   I wanted you to know I was thinking of you.

AUDREY *throws the book down rather casually.*

> I tried to get you back, Audrey, I tried and tried. My
> sister — your aunt wouldn't let me near the house. All
> my letters came back unopened.

AUDREY   A woman in the elevator said the Russians and
the Americans have a new laser gun that can obliterate
anything it points at.

INGRID   I think how fast the last twenty years have gone
by, how easily the next twenty could. If I live past that I'll
be lucky to have someone push me in a wheelchair from
one side of the room to the other. Better I should die and
better now I should live even one year with someone
who says they love me than suffer here like a dog.

AUDREY   I used to wish you were dead because the idea
of you being alive and having left me was so insulting
it was unbearable. Consolation came in knowing you
could never be happy: wherever you'd go, whoever
you'd be with, I would always be there tugging at your
conscience like a nail at a scab. I thought even if I lived
to be one hundred I would always be a deserted seven-
year-old screaming and kicking the walls until I grew
numb or was threatened I'd be stuck in an orphanage
whichever came first, I don't remember, I didn't keep a
diary, there was nothing I wanted to be reminded of or
repeat to others.

INGRID   You want to send me to hell, Audrey, save
              yourself the trouble, I live there now.

AUDREY   Clients would come into my office and flirt with
              me, very attractive men, constantly. I loved rejecting
              them, rejecting everything.

INGRID   As I rejected you.

AUDREY   That's right.

INGRID   And nothing I can say or do will ever change
              that so why talk about it. Nail the lid on it and bury it.

AUDREY   I can't.

INGRID   Walk on me if you think it would help but don't
              talk about it anymore I can't stand it!

AUDREY   It would I think.

INGRID   What?

AUDREY   Walk on you.

INGRID   Literally?

AUDREY   Yes. You walked on me at an age when walking
              on me literally would have been more kind, so I'd be
              letting you off easy if I walked on you.

INGRID   And you'd forgive me, really forgive me if I
              consented, if I let you walk on me?

AUDREY   Yes, yes I believe I would.

Slowly, **INGRID** *lies face down on the floor.*

INGRID   All right, I'm ready. Step on me.

AUDREY *steps up on her mother and walks back and forth all over her with her pink slippers.* INGRID *cries out occasionally with pain. The more* INGRID *cries out the more satisfying it is to* AUDREY. BRUNO *enters with snow on his overcoat.* AUDREY *does not notice him.*

AUDREY   Angels are whirling around me like rings — can you feel their light?! They're near me because I'm carrying one of their little sisters or brothers. I'm so afraid of letting it go because then day by day as the baby gets more and more like us the angels will ascend higher and higher until all I can see are the palms of their feet disappearing up into the ceiling.

BRUNO *takes off his ring and kneels at* AUDREY's *feet.*

BRUNO   The world is a frightening place, Audrey, and things of course could be better. They could be better for everyone but that doesn't mean we have to live like leftovers on a sinking ship. I could be a better man and I'll try to be, I swear it. I'm sorry it's offensive to you when I say I love you. I do love you, Audrey, and I'll work to make that expression mean something for the first time if it's never meant anything before. Please marry me. Say yes, take it and say yes.

INGRID *(Underfoot)* Say yes, Audrey.

Enter NISSIM *with Audrey's suitcase.*

NISSIM   Why are you wearing your coat indoors?

BRUNO   Don't ask me why I'm on one knee or why
Audrey's standing on her mother.

NISSIM   You're proposing marriage and she's making up
with her mother.

BRUNO   Say yes, Audrey, marry me. Take my ring.

NISSIM   Say yes, Audrey, marry him. Take the ring. Take
it. My parents stayed happily married until they knifed
each other. Take the ring. Everyone take what they have
to and go.

BRUNO   I'll never leave you, Audrey.

AUDREY   Yes. Yes.

*BRUNO slips the ring on AUDREY's finger, she steps off her
mother and has a painful contraction.*

BRUNO   Audrey is that your first?

AUDREY   They started this morning.

BRUNO   What! Oh my God where's your suitcase?! *(He
sees it and grabs it)* Thank God your aunt's pacing in the
lobby — she can drive us to the hospital.

AUDREY   I'm having it, oh God, I'm having it. I'm ready,
Nissim, I'm ready, Mommy, Bruno, I'm ready, I'm having
it, I'm ready, I'm ready.

*BRUNO picks up AUDREY and with some difficulty carries
her, her legs somewhat astride, and the suitcase out of the*

apartment. **NISSIM** *looks out the window through the*
Venetian blinds. **INGRID** *doesn't move from the floor. After*
some moments **NISSIM** *lifts the blinds, it is gently snowing.*

NISSIM   It's snowing. Everyone looks so sad and lost in
the snow. Suddenly I'm so tired. Here's your present,
Ingrid. I'll open it for you. *(He opens it, inside the box there*
is a beautiful blue silk scarf. He kneels to show it to her)
It goes in a way with the blouse you wore the day I met
you. I left the price tag on it in case you hated it.

INGRID   You shouldn't have spent so much.

NISSIM   That's the store code, this is the price. *(He*
plugs in the tree. The red lights go on and off, on and off)
The cradle looks so alluring, doesn't it? Do you think it
would break if I got in it? I'm getting in. *(He climbs into*
the cradle. After a moment, in the cradle, face up, pitiless)
I listen to records at the wrong speed and don't know
it. I put quarters in other people's machines at the
laundromat and watch the clothes spin and dry while
mine sit in a wet unattended lump. I'm a tragic character
and the tragedy of it is I have to go on living. If only I
knew there was some curtain to be drawn or light that
could go out and I could go home and be someone else it
would be bearable but I have no place to go and no one
else to be.

INGRID *has picked up her diary, she opens it and reads from it.*

INGRID   Dear Audrey, today I went to the beach and burned my skin. I can't sleep. Yesterday was your birthday and I bought you a flower in the street. I can't concentrate for the clatter of the petals falling on the nighttable near the clock and the breath of the man I love hot on my neck, the sound makes me shiver and I feel as old as the world and I want to call out has anyone ever been so alone? Tomorrow and tomorrow. I want to read this one day and laugh.

She rips out the page, laughs, and weeps, covering her face with the blue scarf. The snow falls. The red tree lights blink. The cradle rocks back and forth. Curtain.

THE END

remembering harry

A tribute to Harry Kondoleon by the playwright **Wendy Wasserstein**, delivered at his memorial on 11th April 1994, at the Public Theater, New York

I met Harry during the production of his play *Christmas on Mars*, which I saw three or four times, at Playwrights Horizons. I was riveted by that play. Maybe it was because towards the end of the second act a mother says to her pregnant daughter, 'Walk on me if you think it would help,' and the daughter replies, 'It would I think.' The stage directions read, 'Audrey steps up on her mother and walks back and forth all over her with her pink slippers.'

And every time I saw that play I thought, 'How did Harry know how much I want to walk on my mother?' How did Harry have the kindness and the sharpness to know that during that walk the mother and daughter would reconcile?

But that was what was so extraordinary about Harry. His ability to be so sharp, so critical, so impossible, and simultaneously be so kind, and so loving, and so deeply, deeply funny.

After the third time Harry saw me loitering the halls after *Christmas on Mars*, he invited me to his home in the East

Village for lunch. I walked to his house, and I looked at the Turkish Russian bath across the street and wondered, 'Good God, does Harry live there?' I rang the bell and after three endless flights of stairs there was Harry elegantly dressed and serving chicken curry and poached pears on perfect blue and white china.

We often had those poached pear lunches and talked about our plays, our mutual love lives, the lack of our mutual love lives. Harry had a great gift for friendship. He considered his friends family, as if we all were part of a larger family of Harry's. I remember when I began writing *The Heidi Chronicles* about a female art historian, Harry began telling me about his sister Christine. It became clear to me that Harry cherished being a brother and took the time to really know a woman friend as a sister. I always felt safe with Harry. I always felt that he knew me very well.

Last year he asked me to his loft to give me a drawing of his. We looked at a few of them and I asked him which one I should take and he took out one that was called 'Born Nasty!!!' I asked him how he knew that was my secret self and he said, 'You wish it was your secret self and that's why you should have it.' I have many favorite moments of Harry. I will never forget the time Harry and I and Bill Finn drove up to Williams College to be on a theatre panel. Harry was talking about Cliff and Tina [his parents], and I was talking about Maurice and Lola, and Billy was talking about Barbara Finn.

And suddenly Harry insisted that we turn down the radio while he recited all of Sylvia Plath's poem 'Daddy.' There we were cruising down the Taconic listening to Harry say 'Daddy.' Or the first time I saw him at St Vincent's Hospital when I found out he was ill, and he said, 'What do you think of the gown? It's Yves Saint Vincent.' This year when Cindy Tolan looked at apartments for him and he would call to say, 'Am I too picky? Cindy saw forty apartments, none of them to my liking.' And when Harry called to thank me for the Christmas dinner I gave with Harry, Bill Finn, Christopher Durang, Paul Rudnick, and Peter Parnell, Harry advised me that I wasn't going to meet a husband this way.

The memory I was thinking of today when I thought of speaking here at the Public was *Zero Positive* playing upstairs and David Pierce running around in that wonderful toga and sandals and how much I loved that play. Like Bob Brustein, I too thought it was a masterpiece. And I remember a conversation we had last summer at Cathy and Stephen Graham's house. Everyone else had gone to the pool to swim and we sat it out. Harry told me he was looking forward to his book being published and he knew Cathy would throw him a simply splendid party. Of course he had specific recommendations to make that party great. Then he began talking about my play and *Angels in America*, and the play that he had just written, and his hope that the theatre would become more important to our culture.

Harry was an extraordinary artist who was constantly producing, throughout his illness he gathered his energies to work.

At Harry's service the other week at the Greek Orthodox Church in Queens I walked in with Cathy and Stephen Graham and Bill Finn and there was Harry's family and friends all seated waiting for the service to begin and there was indeed someone vacuuming. All the Harry fan club, Robyn Goodman, Stephen Soba, Don Shewey, were there and we were all rolling our eyes until Vincent went up and said, 'Stop!' What seemed most extraordinary to me, as it did to Stephen, was it was as if it was all written by Harry Kondoleon. I wish he was here to use it and I hope he is somewhere thrilling where he can use it, and after dine on perfectly poached pears.

I will cherish him, his plays, and what he taught me about friendship.

Wendy Wasserstein was an American playwright. She received the Tony Award for Best Play and the Pulitzer Prize for Drama in 1989 for her play The Heidi Chronicles.

Acknowledgements

Alastair Curtis and Polari Press wish to thank: Don Shewey, Stephen Soba, Christine Kondoleon, Jonathan Lomma and London Performance Studios.

Polari Press

Taking our name from the secret slang Polari, we are an independent publishing house that seeks out hidden voices and helps them be heard.

Although Polari was spoken almost exclusively by gay and bisexual men, the nature of clandestine meetings of the mid-1900s, when homosexuality was still criminalised, brought together people from all walks of life who all had an influence on the language.

Cockney, Romany, and Italian languages mixed with the colloquialisms of thespians, circus performers, wrestlers, sailors, and wider criminal communities to create a slang to express their sexuality secretly and safely.

Inspired by these origins, we publish queer voices as well as other marginalised groups, to share our perspectives with each other and help build a collaborative platform for all of us.

polari.com

Polari Plays

We are creating an active archive for queer-authored play scripts and performance.

For a complete listing of Polari Plays titles, visit:

polari.press/plays

Follow us on social media:

@PolariPress